Isaiah 26:3–4
"PERFECT PEACE XII"

River

VANESSA RAYNER

authorHOUSE®

AuthorHouse™
1663 Liberty Drive
Bloomington, IN 47403
www.authorhouse.com
Phone: 1 (800) 839-8640

Published by AuthorHouse 08/01/2017

ISBN: 978-1-5462-0175-5 (sc)
ISBN: 978-1-5462-0174-8 (e)

Print information available on the last page.

Contents

A Gift . . .

Presented to

_____

From

_____

Date

_____

True Peace Only Comes from the Prince of Peace

It doesn't mean that everything around
you is calm and tranquil;
it means you are able to remain peaceful
during the storms of life.

Theme

The message of **I**saiah **26:3-4** is concerning *"Perfect Peace."* This is the distinct and unifying composition of this book with the subtitle <u>River</u>.

~~~~~~~~~~~~~

You will keep in perfect peace all who trust in you, all whose thoughts are fixed on you! Trust in the LORD always, for the LORD God is the eternal Rock. Isaiah 26:3-4 NLT

Prayer

Oh Heavenly Father,
I just want to say thank you, I love you, so.

I pray that your people are learning to
experience Your "Perfect Peace"
every day, all day and throughout the day.

Father God,
I ask in Jesus' name that the Holy Spirit,
the Comforter,
will help readers to remember Your word from this book.
I pray it will give them peace, and joy
at a time, they need it the most.
And when they think of You and Your word,
they realize that it going to be a lovely day.
You are still on the throne.

Lord, I'm grateful for the assignment,
You given me in Your kingdom work.
I thank You for blessing those that help
make Your work able to go forth.

Father in the Gospel of Matthew and Mark,
You made it clear that You will reward
those that bless your servant.
It could be by prayer, words of
encouragement, to even given
that person a cup of water.

Father God,
I give you all the Glory, Honor and Praise in Jesus' name.
Amen.

~~~~~~~~~~~~

Matthew 10:42 ~~~ Mark 9:41

Author's Notes

Author notes normally provide a way to add extra information to one's book that may be awkward and inappropriate to include in the text of the book itself. It provides supplemental contextual details on the aspects of the book. It can help readers understand the book content and the background details of the book better. The times and dates of researching, reading, and gathering this information are not included; mostly when I typed on it.

0644, Saturday, February 11, 2017; This morning, I woke up with urgency. I had a reoccurring dream that happens two Saturdays ago, I believed. In this dream, there was a figure of a person standing near a narrow river, facing what felt to be north. The figure had it back turned so I couldn't see a face. The figure was wearing a loosely grayish cape with a hood that reaches the ground so I couldn't determine the sex. The narrow river was no more than twelve inch wide. However, it was a beautiful dark deep purplish blue color moving at a steady pace, but on both sides of the river had small noticeable cracks in the riverbanks. The surrounding area was flat with no visible sign of life. There was plenty of daylight, but no sun was shining. The entire scene looked white, except for the figure and river. It felt like I was looking down on this place. So when I dreamed about it, the first time, I prayed. I asked Father who I need to pray for, or for what. For a few days, I pondered on it, wondered about it, told it to a few people, and then prayed about it some more. Several days later, I dreamed about it again. So I started reading about the rivers in the Bible. Now, I dreamt about it last night, too. This is how this book got its title.

0654, Sunday, 12 February 2017; My laptop computer screen goes blank a few seconds after I turned it on. I tried to get the computer screen to come back on, but after 10 minutes or so, I just prayed over it (the computer), and about it (the situation that just happened). Guess I have to use the desk top computer. Hallelujah, in spite of.

*****Try not to laugh to hard . . . smile

It's about 0721 now; I'm walking from room to room looking for my coffee cup to make some more coffee. I go from my dining room back to the living room looking for that coffee cup. Then I leave the living room and goes to my bedroom. In the meantime, in my mind, I'm saying where did I put that cup! I leave the bedroom goes to the bathroom, and then peeks at the kitchen table, and back to the living room, again. I'm standing in the dining room, looking up at the ceiling, trying to think, where I put that cup!!! A few second later, I hear the microwave go ding. I just smiled and verbally said, "Father God this is going to be a very interesting morning, I can see. . . I'm so glad YOU are my Shepherd."

1601; Monday, 13 February 2017;

0702; Tuesday, 14 February 2017; Just typing in a few thoughts before I go to work.

1648; Tuesday, 14 February 2017; Happy Valentine Day!

1706; Wednesday, 15 February 2017

0651; Thursday, 16 February 2017; Printing off a little something, something to read over, today . . . *smile*

1643; Thursday, 16 February 2017

1739; Friday, 17 February 2017

1455; Saturday, 18 February 2017; My laptop computer is working, now. It's a miracle. Early this morning, I'm first and only person in Best Buy Geek Squat computer repair line. The service tech started telling me all the possible problems with the computer. He didn't hook any test equipment to it. When he said it would be around $384.00 to repair it along with the antivirus software, I said ok. Then he stated it would be another $100.00 to remove pictures from my hard drive if the hard drive is bad. I said, let me cancel this repair. I need to step back and think about this. He tried to get me to change my mind, but I wouldn't. I told him, I need to figure out do I want to repair it or buy a new one. When I left Best Buy, I decided to take this computer to a computer repair shop, down the street over the expressway. The name is Uptech Computer Repair, and the tech name I believe is Stephan. When the computer tech plugged the computer into the outlet, and push the on button, it started up. I said, you much have that magic touch. We both laugh, but my soul was saying Hallelujah. He turned it off and turned it on again with no problem. I tired giving him $20, but he said that's alright. I thanked him out loud and Father God in my inner being.

0813; Sunday, 19 February 2017

2040; Monday, 20 February 2017; President's Day

0800; Saturday, 25 February 2017

0504; Sunday, 26 February 2017

2002; Wednesday, 01 March 2017; He's Sweet I Know . . .

0554; Sunday, 05 March 2017

1809; Sunday, 05 March 2017; Finally, went to Sunday School at Bellevue Baptist Church and it was great! "The God Who Whispers" 1 Kings 19:1-18

1901; Monday, 06 March 2017

0606; Saturday, 25 March 2017: Happy Birthday too me! Thank You Father!

0526; Saturday, 01 April 2017

0628; Sunday, 02 April 2017

0533; Thursday, 13 April 2017; Off work with a painful sprain upper thigh muscle. God is good all the time; All the time God is good! Hallelujah!!!

1817; Friday, 14 April 2017; Good Friday

1644; Sunday, 16 April 2017; Easter Sunday

0617; Friday, 21 April 2017; Father God is good all the time. The painful sprain upper thigh muscle issue started back Tuesday, at work. I had to leave work; it had me basically stuck in motion, at times. Three times my assigned Resident Clerk where I work had to help keep me from falling until staff arrived with a vehicle. I decided to go home instead of the ER. About 0115, early Wednesday morning I was taken to the ER by Larry. ER doctor discovered that the medication I had just started taking for my high cholesterol on March 27, 2017, was causing the severe upper thigh muscles spasm pain which had moved to my waist, back of my thigh, and down to my leg. I had to start walking with a cane, and every step was painful. I'm still walking with a cane at the moment; but the spasm and pain have subsided, quite a bit, and I thank Father for that. Hallelujah! I'm off work until Monday, April 24, 2017, hoping by then the Atorvastatin had cleared out my body, enough for me to function normally; that's one of the side effects of this medication. Yesterday, I walked around my house in pain with my cane thanking God, praising the Lord, and calling on the name of Jesus while quoting The Word of God. He's my EVERYTHING! I don't understand everything, but I trust HIM in and through everything. Today, I feel good enough to work on His book. Praise God Saints!

0628; Sunday, 23 April 2017; Yesterday morning, I pressed my way down to Crawford, MS to attend my cousin funeral, "Mack Arthur Brooks" at Charity Mission Full Gospel Baptist Church. Rev. DeMarrio Brown, the Pastor at Christian Faith M.B. Church in Starkville, MS preached the Eulogy. It was HOLY GHOST AWESOME!!! I felt the power of God in his message. I felt chills all over my body from the crown of my head to the sole of my feet, some people would call it goose bumps; I call it "The Anointing." I claimed my healing in the process. I didn't feel the need for my cane anymore, haven't taken a muscle relaxer or pain pill since, and I can only recall having one muscle spasm while driving back to Memphis by myself; I just kept claiming my deliverance. Rev. DeMarrio Brown preached with the Anointing of the Holy Spirit, I could write a book on what he preached on. Nevertheless, I will touch on a few POWERFUL points he mentioned in the Eulogy.

1. We don't grieve like people who have no hope.
2. Jesus died for our sins; He was buried and was raised to life again for us.
3. Jesus will return with the believers who had died.
4. Jesus will come down from heaven with a commanding shout.
5. The believers who have died will rise from the graves, first.
6. The believers on the earth will be caught up in the clouds to meet the Lord.
7. Encourage each other with words.
8. The Resurrection of Christ
9. The Resurrection of the Dead
10. We live by faith, not by sight.
11. When we are absent from the body, we are present with the Lord.
12. Praise God in all circumstances; in sickness and in wellness.

Hallelujah is the Highest Praise!

0511; Saturday, 29 April 2017

1359; Monday, 08 May 2017

2006; Tuesday, 09 May 2017

1931; Wednesday, 10 May 2017

1917; Thursday, 11 May 2017

0656; Saturday, 13 May 2017

1529; Monday, 15 May 2017

1908; Tuesday, 17 May 2017

0625; Saturday, 20 May 2017

0118; Sunday, 21 May 2017

0828; Monday, 29 May 2017; Memorial Day

0842; Sunday, 04 June 2017; Lord, when am I going to learn!!! Help me accept it is what it is . . .

1522; Monday, 05 June 2017

1651; Tuesday, 06 Jun. 2017

1749; Thursday, 08 June 2017

0650; Saturday, 10 June 2017; Yesterday, I traveled to St. Louis, MO., to attend Stanley Brian Fields' funeral, my cousin's on my mother side of the family. Pastor Carl Smith was the Officiant. He preached from the last chapter, of the last book of the Bible. It was captivating and soul touching. The message begins with "And I saw a new heaven and a new earth…" Hallelujah!

0650; Sunday, 11 June 2017

0550; Monday, 12 June 2017

1650; Wednesday, 14 June 2017; Happy Birthday Big Brother! AD Moore

1652; Thursday, 15 June 2017

0548; Saturday, 17 June 2017

0659; Sunday, 18 June 2017

1740; Monday, 19 June 2017

1919; Tuesday, 20 June 2017

2103; Wednesday, 21 June 2017

2352; Saturday, 24 June 2017

0000; Sunday, 25 June 2017

1646; Friday, 07 July 2017; Proofreading Time!

My oldest son Alvin from Seattle, Washington, and his lady friend Claudia have been in town since July 3, 2017. Enjoying the company to the max. Today, they going to his father's family reunion "Meet-and-Greet Gathering" in Blytheville, Arkansas.

0636; Saturday, 08 July 2017; Around 0908, I just finished eyeballing 72 pages, and "The God Who Whispers" keep stirring in my spirit. Glory be to God!

0914; Sunday, 09 July 2017

2041; Monday, 10 July 2017

1503; Sunday, 16 July 2017; Need to finish proof-reading. Just got back from the Mobley's Family Reunion in Starkville, MS which started Friday night with a banquet. It was wonderful! Mrs. Elvie Mobley the oldest living family member. She is 99 years old. What a blessing!

2003; Monday, 17 July 2017; Will be concentrating on Chapter 8 and 9, tonight.

1921; Tuesday, 18 July 2017

1938; Wednesday, 19 July 2017; Happy Birthday, Mom! (Ulyer Moore) I love you and miss you, so very much. I'm going to send AuthorHouse this manuscript tonight.

Preface

Isaiah 26:3-4, "Perfect Peace XII" ~ River

The book, <u>Isaiah 26:3-4, "Perfect Peace XII" River</u> is the 12th book in a series called Isaiah 26:3-4, "Perfect Peace." LORD, I Bless Your Holy Name! Hallelujah is the Highest Praise.

It all started from how I drew near to the LORD in my workplace by keeping my mind on Him. I related numbers, you see throughout the day, everywhere, on almost everything on Him, His word, biblical events, and facts to give me peace in the midst of chaos.

It's our desire for you to discover the power of the Holy Spirit by numbers, words, places, people, and things related to a river or rivers.

Remember, the LORD Jesus <u>PROMISED us tribulation</u> while we were in this world.

These things, I have spoken unto you,
that in me ye might have peace.
In the world ye shall have tribulation:
But be of good cheer; I have overcome the world.
John 16:33 KJV

However, we have been <u>PROMISED His peace</u> while we endure these trials, tribulations, troubles, and tests. Perfect Peace is given only to those whose mind and heart reclines upon the LORD. God's peace is increased in us according to the knowledge of His Holy Word.

> **Grace and peace be multiplied unto you**
> **through the knowledge of God,**
> **and of Jesus our LORD.**
> *2* Peter 1:2 KJV

Thanks

To the Readers . . .

As a disciple of the LORD Jesus Christ, I have learned true success comes when we are seeking and striving to do God's purpose for our lives. Our real happiness lies in doing God's will; not in fame and fortune.

On behalf of our Heavenly Father's Ministry, I want to thank you for your support. Thanks for helping me spread "Perfect Peace" through your e-mail, Facebook, Twitter, LinkedIn, Instagram, Tumblr, and etc. accounts to your family, friends, neighbors, co-workers, church family, internet social friends, and associates.

Remember, you may not know until you get to heaven just how much a song you sung, kind words spoken by you or even a book you suggested reading, at the right moment, encourage a person to keep on going when a few minutes before they were tempted to give up on life and their walk with the LORD.

I greatly appreciate your love and kindness to this ministry.

Acknowledgements

First and foremost, I wish to express my sincere gratitude to *"Our Heavenly Father"* for his guidance, patience, and lovingkindness throughout the writing of this book.

I would like to thank Larry D. Rayner, who encourages and lift me up more than he realizes with his daily inspirational text message, which he also sent to others.

Introduction

For Those Who Want To Be Kept In "Perfect Peace"

This book was prepared and written to open your mind to a "Perfect Peace" that comes only from God. I'm striving to elevate you into a "Unique and Profound" awareness of God's presence around you at all time.

According to some people, it's hard to keep your mind on the LORD. While most Christians will agree that if you keep your mind stayed on the LORD, He will keep you in "Perfect Peace." This is why so many people enjoy going to church on Sundays and attending midweek services for peace and joy that they receive, but only for a short time.

You can experience the peace of the LORD throughout the day and every day. His unspeakable joy, his strength, his "Perfect Peace" in the midst of the storm whether it's at work, home, college, school, etc. You can also experience this peace, even when your day is going well.

This concept of this book was placed in my spirit by our Father, which art in heaven, to help me when he allowed Satan to test me at my workplace until he finished molding me into a MAP; (Minister/Ambassador/Pastor).

Throughout these pages, I will be focussing on biblical events, and facts surrounding "rivers" and "water bodies." However, I am sure much more can be said on this word, so these examples serve merely as an introduction and are not exhaustive by any means.

Dedication

This book is dedicated to those that protect America's rivers, lakes, ponds, seas, oceans, and streams.

The Nature Conservancy Staff
United States Army Corps of Engineers
Last by not least . . .
The Volunteers

Chapter 1

RIVERS & STREAMS

What is the difference between lakes, oceans, and seas? Do the words "river" and "stream" refer to the same body of water? What are other names for watercourses or bodies of water?

Water is what our planet depends on. It is found in abundance, and nearly 3/4th of the earth is covered with water bodies that are either; huge, big or small. The vast, almost boundless oceans cover approximately 71% of earth's surface. These continuous water bodies contain saline water and house a mass variety of marine species. Other watercourses and water bodies that are commonly found all over the world are lakes, rivers, streams, and seas.

Notes of Interest: Bodies of water or water bodies are considered any significant accumulation of water. This term commonly refers to oceans, seas, and lakes. It also includes smaller pools of water such as ponds, wetland or puddles. Watercourses are natural or artificial channels through which a body of water flows. These include rivers, streams, anabranches, and canals.

~~~~~~~~~~~~

Rivers and streams account for the majority of watercourses used by humanity. Even though the words "river" and "stream" are considered interchangeable, they are not the same. If there are no streams, rivers cannot be formed.

There are several differences between rivers and streams. Streams are small water bodies that exist by themselves but when they come together creates a small or large river. Most streams are shallow water bodies, and some streams are so small that one can easily walk across it or see and pick up an object that is accidentally dropped in it. Even though, some streams carry a smaller amount of water, they can be very turbulent when the water falls from great heights. Streams are usually more turbulent and aggressive than rivers. When two streams meet, the smaller one is called a tributary.

A stream might flow within a small and narrow bank but they are known to have great erosion powers. Streams have been known to erode stones, sculpt the surface of the earth and take the sediment into the rivers that later carry it to oceans and lakes. In some areas of the world, a stream is also known as a creek. This term is mainly used in North American, Australia, and New Zealand.

There are several types of streams such as Headwater stream, Year-round Stream, Seasonal Streams, and Rain-dependent Streams. Headwater Streams are the beginnings of rivers. Year-round Streams are the streams that flow throughout the year without a problem. The Seasonal Streams flow only during the time where there is enough water. Rain-dependent Streams have rain water as their main source of water supply.

The place, where many streams meet to form a large water body is called a river, referred to as confluence. The vast majority of rivers originate in hills and mountains. Some rivers originate in mountains and flow downwards under the action of gravity. They can be violent and turbulent, carving out their own course carrying sand and stone that form sediment in areas down the mountains.

Some rivers are formed as a result of melting glaciers. The melting snow runs down the mountains in the shape of multiple streams. They meet at a confluence where the water body becomes large and gets transformed into a river. These rivers are an excellent source of freshwater, frequently deeper than streams and finally drain into larger water bodies such as lakes, seas or oceans. Unlike, streams, rivers flow in wider water banks, but they both have water currents. The currents are what moves sediment, debris, and objects.

The main component that decides whether a waterway is a river or stream is the size. Streams and rivers are both essential for our survival, but according to the <u>Stream Order Classification of Waterways</u>, a watercourse that is between sixth and twelfth order is considered a river. The world's largest river, the Amazon River is of the twelfth order.

Lakes are another water body formed with freshwater of a river and are surrounded by land on all sides. A lake contains freshwater that is not moving, it's still. Lakes are big and small, and they are mostly formed by rivers in basin area at the foot of mountains and hills. Most lakes contain the water that does not drain in oceans. Lakes are fed by rivers and can dry up when rivers do not drain into them. Lakes are not permanent. Some places that have lakes today were dry hundreds of years ago and some lakes of today may disappear over time.

Oceans are considered the largest water bodies on earth. **Let's name them . . .**

1. _____
2. _____
3. _____
4. _____

Answer in back of book

The oceans water is very salty and home to numerous types of marine species. Oceans have an average depth of 2.7 miles. Though the oceans are divided into four, in reality, they are one massive water body covering more than 70% of earth's surface. The boundaries of these oceans are not clear. Some of these oceans have been divided into smaller water bodies known as seas.

Seas are generally referred to a large body of salt water connected with an ocean. The word "sea" is commonly used as a synonym for oceans. The Pacific Ocean is the largest ocean which covers 64,186,000 square miles. The largest sea is Mediterranean with an area of 1,144,800 square miles. Even the world's smallest ocean, the Arctic Ocean is bigger than the Mediterranean Sea. The top largest seas are Mediterranean, Caribbean, South China, Bering, Gulf of Mexico and Okhotsk.

Chapter 2

THE GARDEN
OF EDEN

The events in the Bible take place over a large geographic area, and it covers approximately 3,600 years of history. The geographic area in the Bible ranges from Egypt to Ethiopia, Israel through Mesopotamia, and Greece to Rome. The Bible uses bodies of water to identify an area or location where events took place.

The types of "bodies of water" mentioned in the Bible are listed below. To my surprise, ocean(s) is not mentioned in the KJV.

1.	River	217 times	Begins at Genesis 2:10
2.	Rivers	71 times	Begins at Exodus 7:19
3.	Sea	352 times	Begins at Genesis 1:26
4.	Seas	25 times	Begins at Genesis 1:10
5.	Brook	37 times	Begins at Genesis 32:23
6.	Brooks	13 times	Begins at Numbers 21:14
7.	Stream	12 times	Begins at Numbers 21:15
8.	Streams	12 times	Old Testament Only; Begins at Exodus 7:19
9.	Pond	0	

10.	Ponds	3 times	Begins at Exodus 7:19
11.	Lake	10 times	New Testament Only (Luke & Revelation)
12.	Lakes	0	
13.	Creek	1 times	Acts 27:39
14.	Creeks	0	
15.	Ocean	0	
16.	Oceans	0	

Notes of Interest: Often the same body of water in the Bible will have multiple names. Ancient scrolls indicate that when different Kings capture a territory, there were tendencies to change the name of the villages, town, cities or rivers. Some scholars will use the original names for water sources in the Bible, while other water sources appear different in various biblical translations.

~~~~~~~~~~~~

The Garden of Eden is often called Paradise. It's the biblical garden of God, described in Genesis, chapters 2 and 3. According to the Bible, a river flowed from the Garden of Eden to water the garden, and from there it divided into four rivers.

The first river is named the Pishon. The only mention of the word "Pishon" is found in the Book of Genesis. It's the river that flowed around the whole land of Havilah, where there is gold. The gold of that land is good bdellium and onyx stones, Genesis 2:10-12. The first river signifies the intelligence of the faith that is from love.

The Hebrew root word for "Pishon" is "puwsh" which means "scatter, press on, break loose or spring forward" is where it gets its name from. It is impossible to determine where the Pishon River flowed during the pre-flood era. Scientists debate that the Pishon River could be the Nile, the Indus, or the Ganges River.

The Garden of Eden prepared by God was not only bountiful, but it was also beautiful. The Garden of Eden was a place rich with life-giving water, and the land was lavished with precious metals and jewels. Furthermore, the Pishon River along with the other three rivers eventually marked the boundaries of the land promised to Abraham by the Lord, Genesis 15:18.

The second river is named "Gihon," and this river flows through the land of Cush. The word "Gihon" means "bursting forth." The second river of Paradis compasses the whole land of Cush. The second river signifies the knowledge of all things that belong to the good and the true. Cush was the first son of Ham, who was a son of Noah. He was the brother of Canaan, Mizraim and Phut and the father of Nimrod, Sabtecah, Sabtah, Raamah, Havilah and Seba, Genesis 10:6 and 1 Chronicles 1:10.

The third river in the Garden of Eden is called the Tigris. The word "Tigris" means "rapid." It flows to the east of Asshur, and south from the mountains of Turkey through Iraq and empties itself into the Persian Gulf. The third river refers to reason or the clear-sightedness of reason.

Asshur and the more recognizable Assyria are actually from the same Hebrew word, which means level or straight. Asshur was a grandson of Noah, the son of Noah's son Shem.

The Hiddekel River flows east of Asshur. It is generally identified as the Tigris River. Hiddekel is a Hebrew word, and it is mentioned again in Daniel 10:4. The Hiddekel River is known as the Idiklat or Diklat River in Assyrian, and as the Tigra River in Old Persian.

The fourth river is the Garden of Eden is the Euphrates which means fruitfulness. The root of the word "Euphrates" is "Pehrate" which means "to break forth and abound." The Euphrates river signifies memory-knowledge and the exciting things from which this knowledge come.

The Euphrates River is the largest river in Southwestern Asia; about 1780 miles long. The Euphrates River Valley is regarded as the cradle of civilization. It was considered by the Hebrews as the north-eastern boundary of Israel, 1 King 4:21. It was the western boundary of Mesopotamia which divided it from the "Land of Hatti," which included all the land between the Euphrates and the Mediterranean. The Babylon bordered this river, as the Nineveh bordered the Tigris River. It flowed by the ancient city of Carchemish, 2 Chronicles 35:20.

The Euphrates River banks overflow every year and rise as high as 12 feet during the months of March, April, May because of the melting of the snow. Today, the Tigris and Euphrates have the same names and are still located in the proximity. However, there is much uncertainty concerning Pishon and Gihon river locations. Scientists have discovered that there are many flowing, and dry river beds near the Tigris and Euphrates Rivers, but it is hard to identify the two lost rivers. Many times, names of rivers change over time as they dry up, and are forgotten.

Out of the four rivers mentioned in the Garden of Eden, the Euphrates River is the only river mentioned in the New Testament. Twice, the Euphrates River is mentioned in the Book of Revelation, regarding a prophecy that predicts thing to occur just before Jesus returns. When the last days is threatening the existence of life on earth, the Apostle John says:

> **"And the sixth angel poured out his vial**
> **upon the great river Euphrates;**
> **and the water thereof was dried up,**
> **that the way of the kings of the**
> **east might be prepared."**
> Revelation 16:12 KJV

Chapter 3

WADI

The Hebrew word for river is "Na'hawr" which includes the sea. The word "river" is used in the Bible to refer to all kinds of watercourses. A watercourse is a channel that a flowing body of water follows which also includes those rivers which are dried-up for part of the year or a season. Other watercourses mentioned in the Bible are springs, permanent rivers, canals, and wadis.

The word "river" is mentioned in 145 verses in the King James Bible, and in some of those verses, the word is mentioned twice or even three times. The word "rivers" is mentioned in 71 verses of the King James Bible.

In the same day the Lord made a covenant with Abram, saying,
Unto thy seed have I given this land,
from the river of Egypt unto the great river,
the river Euphrates:
Genesis 15:18 KJV

In the Bible, dried-up desert riverbeds are called wadis. The single form of the word "wadi" is also spelled "wady." Wadi is the Arabic and Hebrew term used largely in Arab countries. There are 22 Arab countries. The KJV Bible mentions six of the twenty-two countries, and they are listed below; the others are in the back of the book.

1. Egypt
2. Jordan
3. Lebanon
4. Libya
5. Palestine
6. Syria

The Jabbok River in the Bible is considered a wadi. The Jabbok River is also called the Zarqa River. The Jabbok River originates on the east side of the mountain of Gilead and flows about 70 miles. It flows through a deep and broad valley down into the Jordan River, taking no account of its countless water windings.

The Jabbok River is the second largest tributary of the lower Jordan River. A tributary is a freshwater stream that flows into a larger body of water, for example; a stream, river or lake. A tributary doesn't flow directly into the ocean or sea. The Jabbok River rises in the springtime in the city of Amman, also known as ancient Rabbath-Ammon.

Notes of Interest: Today, the city of Amman is considered a major tourist destination in the region. Amman is the capital and most populated city of Jordan which is located in north-central Jordan. It was initially built on 7 hills but now spans over 19 hills. East Amman is predominantly filled with historic sites, while West Amman is more modern. The name "Amman" traces back to "Ammon." The "royal city" that was captured by King

David's General, Joab, 2 Samuel 12:26. King David sent Uriah the Hittite to his death in battle before the walls of the city so he could marry his wife, Bathsheba, 2 Samuel 11:14-27. She was pregnant with King David's child while she was still married to Uriah. Solomon, the son of King David, had Ammonite wives in which one was the mother of Rehoboam, Solomon's successor as king of Judah.

~~~~~~~~~~~~

In earlier Bible history, the Jabbok River marked the boundary between the territory of the Ammonites and King Og, the King of Bashan, but later was an Israel territory boundary.

The Jabbok River forms a natural boundary separating the territory of Reuben and Gad from that of Ammon, Deuteronomy 3:16. Ammon was recorded as lying along the Jabbok River, according to Numbers 21:24, Deuteronomy 2:37, Joshua 12:2. The Jabbok River was the northern boundary of the territory of Sihon the Amorite, according to Numbers 21:24 and Joshua 12.2.

The Jabbok River is mentioned seven times and only in the Old Testament. The first biblical reference to the river occurs in connection with Jacob, who cross the Jabbok River on his way to meet Esau, following his departure from Haran, Genesis 32:22.

**During the night Jacob got up and took his two wives,
his two servant wives,
and his eleven sons and crossed the
Jabbok River with them.**
Genesis 32:22 NLT

The Jabbok River is the meeting place of Jacob and Esau, his twin brother. The Jabbok River is the place where Jacob wrestled with the Lord. His struggle took place at Peniel a ford of the Jabbok River which is considered consecrated, now. The Jabbok River is where Jacob made his total surrender to God. It is where he got his new character, and a new name; Israel.

Remember, Jacob began to send waves of gifts to his brother Esau because he feared Esau and his army of men. Jacob then took his family across the Jabbok River, but he spent the night alone on the opposite side of the Jabbok River. That same night a "man" wrestled with Jacob until daybreak. Jacob told the man, "I will not let you go unless you bless me." The man touched the socket of Jacob's hip, and it became wrenched. Jacob's name was changed to "Israel." Jacob named the place Peniel because he said he saw God face to face, and yet his life was spared," Genesis 32:30.

**And Jacob was left alone,
and there wrestled a man with him
until the breaking of the day.**
Genesis 32:24 KJV

The word "Jabbok" means "a place of passing over," it stands for "struggle," and portrays "a lonely place." Our own Jabbok must be faced alone. It has been said, "You can cross the Red Sea with a mighty host of the redeemed who leaves Egypt, cross the Jordan River with the victorious army of the Lord, but you will cross Jabbok River alone!" This is a private struggle between you and the Lord; no pastors, no family, no friends. Our Jabbok is where God deals with us about our sins and our very own character.

The Jabbok River area was very significant in later Israelite history, as well. After the death of Saul, his son Ish-Bosheth took refuge and ruled from Mahanaim, 2 Samuel 2:8-10. During Absalom's revolt against David; King David fled to Mahanaim, 2 Samuel 17:24-29. Mahanaim seems to be a Transjordan administrative center. Jeroboam I built his Transjordan capital at Peniel; the region east of Jordan River that now forms the central part of Jordan, 1 Kings 12:25-33.

Notes of Interest: Transjordan is an area east of the Jordan River in the Southern Levant which refers to the lower half of the Levant. The lower half of the Levant includes Israel, Palestine, Jordan, Lebanon, southern Syria and the Sinai Desert. The prefix "trans" is Latin and means "across" or beyond. Therefore, "Transjordan" refers to the land on the other side of the Jordan River.

~~~~~~~~~~~~

Chapter 4

THE NILE RIVER

One of the greatest rivers from the Bible perspective is approximately 4,160 miles long. It's also the oldest and longest river in the world that flows northward through eastern Africa into the Mediterranean Sea. It's the Nile River. Most people associate the Nile River with Egypt, but only 1/5 of the river actual runs through the country.

Unique features about the Nile River are listed below:

1. The Nile River flows north, which is the opposite direction of most rivers.
2. The reeds that grew on the banks of the Nile River were used to make boats for the Egyptians.
3. The Ancient Egyptians god for the Nile River was god Hapi, and they routinely made sacrifices to it, so that they would get a flood every year.
4. The Egyptians wanted the Nile River to flood because this was the only way that the soil around the river would become fertilize enough to support the growth of crops.

The word "Nile" is not explicitly mentioned in the King James Bible or the New King James Bible Translations. The Nile River was referred to in the Old Testament as the following:

1. Sihor in Isaiah 23:3 and Jeremiah 2:18

   And by great waters the seed of Sihor,
   the harvest of the river,
   is her revenue; and she is a mart of nations.
   Isaiah 23:3 KJV

2. The River, Genesis 41:1 and Exodus 1:22

   And it came to pass at the end of two full years,
   that Pharaoh dreamed:
   and, behold, he stood by the river.
   Genesis 41:1 KJV

3. The "flood of Egypt" in Amos 8:8

   Shall not the land tremble for this,
   and every one mourn that dwelleth therein?
   And it shall rise up wholly as a flood;
   and it shall be case out and drowned,
   as by the flood of Egypt.
   Amos 8:8 KJV

The KJV Translation uses in place of the word "Nile" the following word or phrase "Sihor," "the river," and "flood of Egypt." Refers to the Nile River is only mentioned in the Old Testament.

Notes of Interest: Although the word "Nile" is not written in the King James Bible or the New King James Bible translation, it is written in other Bible Translations; some of them are listed below.

1. NIV   New International   Dynamic
            Version   Equivalence

2.	NLT	New Living Translation	Paraphrase
3.	ASV	American Standard Version	Formal Equivalent
4.	MSG	The Message	Paraphrase
5.	CEV	Contemporary English Version	Dynamic Equivalence
6.	AMP	Amplified Bible	Formal Equivalent
7.	ESV	English Standard Version	Formal Equivalent
8.	NASB	New American Standard Bible	Formal Equivalent

~~~~~~~~~~~~

Question: Do you remember the different between the translations? Which translation is sometimes called "word-for-word" or "thought-for-thought?" Functional equivalent is known as which translation? You will find the answers in my book titled: Isaiah 26:3-4 "Perfect Peace" The Last Single-Digit; Author Vanessa Buckhalter; published 02/13/2012.

Smile Smile Smile

~~~~~~~~~~~

The Nile River consists of two rivers which are the White Nile and the Blue Nile. The Blue Nile begins at Lake Tana in Ethiopia, while the White Nile begins from Eastern Africa and later joins the Blue Nile in Khartoum, the capital city of Sudan. The Blue Nile is the shorter of the two branches, with a length of 900 miles.

The Nile River starts to rise about the end of June. It rises about 24 feet at Cairo near the end of September and falls by the middle of May. It's said, "If the river rises six feet higher than 24 feet; it's devastation or if the river is six feet lower than 24 feet; it's destitution."

The Nile River Valley in Egypt played a critical role in the history of ancient Egypt. It was the site of the world's first great civilization. The Nile River is the only river in Egypt. The name comes from the Greek word "Nellos" which means valley.

The Nile River plays a prominent role in the early events in the life of Moses in Exodus. Moses name comes from his experience with the Nile River. Moses named means "drawn out of the river." He was a Hebrew baby that was pulled out of the River Nile and adopted by the Egyptian Pharaoh's daughter.

In brief, before Moses was born, the children of Israel were living in slavery in Egypt. Pharaoh was afraid of their growing population, during that time. He placed all of the Hebrews under extreme bondage so they could not rebel against him.

The Hebrew population kept increasing, and Pharaoh later placed an order to have all of the male Hebrew babies under the age of two to be killed. It during this time Moses was born. When Moses was born his mother hid him for 3 months, so he would not be killed. After 3 months, his mother placed him in an ark made out of bulrushes, and then placed him down by the reeds along the Nile River banks hoping someone else would find him and raise him up safely. The daughter of Pharaoh found the baby when she went down to the Nile River to take a bath and raised him as her son.

Question: Who were Moses biology parents?

Answer in back of book

Some of the Ten Plagues at the time of the Exodus happened to, and around the Nile River.

Let's name the Ten Plagues:

1. Nile turned to Blood
2. _____
3. G_____
4. F_____
5. Death of Livestock
6. _____
7. _____
8. Locust
9. D_____
10. Death of the Firstborn

Answer in back of book

Throughout history, Egyptians lived by or near the Nile River. The Nile River has been irrigating the valley deserts of Egypt since the dawn of history. On the Nile's western banks, Pharaohs constructed many of their tombs. In the north, during the Old Kingdom Period, royalty and nobility constructed pyramids in the desert sands. The Pyramids on the Giza Plateau is the oldest. It was built long before the Israelites entered Egypt. It is believed that Abraham, Jacob, Joseph, Moses, Joshua, Jeremiah and even baby Jesus saw them.

Ancient Egyptians built most of their cities on the Nile's east bank because this was the side from which the sun arose every morning. On the west bank, where the sun disappeared every night, the Egyptians built their cemeteries, royal tombs, and mortuary temples. The royal tombs of Egypt were built of stone or carved into stone which was costly. Most houses, even palaces were made of sun-dried mud bricks, which was much more available and cheaper than stone. The Israelites were forced into slavery and forced to make mud-brick for the Egyptians' pyramid projects, Exodus 5:6-18.

Ancient Egypt totals almost 400,000 square miles, only the Nile River Valley has been continually inhabited. In prehistoric times, there were two kingdoms called the Upper Egypt which was the south, and Lower Egypt which was considered the north. Both kingdoms were represented by different colored crowns. Upper Egypt was represented by a white crown, and Lower Egypt was represented by a red crown.

It was around 3100 BC when King Menes of Upper Egypt united these two kingdoms. For the next 3,000 years, Egypt was one kingdom with 30 dynasties of Pharaohs. Many

Biblical events were influenced by Egypt, but only four Pharaohs are identified in the Bible, and they are listed below:

1. Shishak, 22nd Dynasty   1 Kings 14:25-26
2. Tirhakah, 25th Dynasty   Isaiah 37:9
3. Necho II, 26th Dynasty   2 Kings 23:9
4. Hophra, 26th Dynasty   Jeremiah 44:30

The history of the Egyptian is divided into three major kingdom periods which are the Old, Middle, and New. During the Old Kingdom Period (2686-2181BC), the pyramids and Great Sphinx were built. Joseph entered Egypt and rose to power during the Middle Kingdom Period (2134-1690 BC), and in the New Kingdom Period (1549-1069), Moses was born, and later led the Exodus.

Biblical events in Egypt occur almost in Lower Egypt, where the Israelites settled in Goshen, the eastern delta. The Bible mentions that the Israelites lived in "Goshen," Genesis 45:10, and "the region of Rameses," Genesis 47:11 during the Sojourn.

The patriarchs Abraham, Joseph, Jacob, and Moses all lived in the Eastern Delta. The Eastern Delta of the Nile is the Land of Goshen. It's the area named in the Bible as the place in Egypt given to the Hebrews by the pharaoh of Joseph, Genesis 45:1-10. It also the land from which the Hebrew later left Egypt with Moses as their leader, at the time of the Exodus.

Chapter 5

THE JORDAN RIVER

The Jordan River flows between the countries of Jordan and Israel. It's one of the most popular rivers in the Bible. The name "Jordan" is derived from the Hebrew word "Yarden, and it is pronounced "yar-dane." The Hebrew word "Yarden" has several meanings which are "descender," "one who descends," and "to flow down." The New Testament Greek word for Jordan is "Iordanis," and it is pronounced "ee-or-dan-ace." The name "descender" is considered an appropriate name for the river because it runs its course from the heights near Mount Hermon to the depths of the Dead Sea.

Notes of Interest: Mount Hermon in the winter is covered with snow. It is located in the highest point in Israel and covers an area of 5,000 acres. Mount Hermon stands about 2814 meters above sea levels. In Bible day, it is believed that it was 4,000 meters above sea levels; 13,000 feet; 2.48 miles high. In the Book of Matthew, Jesus told His disciples that He would die in Jerusalem and rise again at the foot of Mount Hermon, Matthew 16:21-24. Then six days later, Jesus led Peter, James, and John to a high mountain, Matthew 17:1. There, Jesus appearance changed,

His face shone like the sun, and His clothes became dazzling white. It is believed the Transfiguration of Jesus occurred somewhere on Mount Hermon.

~~~~~~~~~~~~

The Jordan River exists in three sections. It begins in the north from the following river sources; the Bareighit, the Hasbany from Mount Hermon, the Leddan, the Banias then runs into Lake Huleh. The Jordan River then flows for about 10 miles from Lake Huleh to the Sea of Galilee in Galilee. Jordan River third section comes from the Sea of Galilee, and then it flows straight about 65 miles into the Dead Sea.

The elevation of the Jordan River drops tremendously, from the north of Israel to the south, passing through the Seas of Galilee in the north, and then it continues to its final destination at the Dead Sea in the South. The drop is about 2,380 feet from the heights of Mount Hermon to the depths of the Dead Sea. Due to Jordan winding course, the river itself actually measures nearly 200 miles.

The Jordan River played a significant role in numerous events over several thousand years in Bible History. The first mention of the Jordan River is when Abraham and Lot parted company in Genesis.

Lot looked around and saw
that the whole plain of Jordan toward
Zoar was well watered,
like the garden of the Lord, like the land of Egypt.

(This was before the Lord destroyed
Sodom and Gomorrah.)
Genesis 13:10 NIV

In Genesis 32, beginning at verse 22, Jacob rose up during the night. He took his two wives (Leah and Rachel), his two women servants (Zilpah the servant of Rachel, and Bilhad the servant of Leah) along with his eleven sons and sent them across the Jordan River at the Jabbok River's ford. The ford is the shallow part of the river. Jacob was left alone at the camp, and a Man wrestled with him until dawn. There Jacob's hip was knocked out of it joint at the socket, and his name was changed from Jacob to Israel at the ford of the Jabbok River which is a tributary of the Jordan River.

When Joshua succeeded Moses as the leader of the people, it was near the end of their Wilderness Journey. The Israelites later entered the Promised Land by crossing the Jordan River, just like the crossing of the Red Sea which was miraculously divided for them. Beginning at Joshua 3:1-17, Joshua got up early the next morning along with the Israelites and left Shittim. When the people came to the Jordan River, they camped there for three days before crossing the Jordan River. The Jordan's banks were overflowing because it was harvest season. The priests carried the ark of the promise went ahead of the people. When they came to the edge of the banks of the Jordan River, they set foot in the water, and the water stopped flowing. The water rose up like a dam as far as the city of Adam near Zarethan and the water flowing down toward the Sea of the Plains also known as the Dead Sea was completely cut off. The people then crossed from the east side of the Jordan River. The priests stood firmly with the ark of the promise on dry ground in the middle of the Jordan River until the whole nation of Israel had crossed the Jordan River.

Gideon came to the Jordan River and crossed over, he and the 300 men who were with him, exhausted yet pursuing the enemies; Zebah and Zalmunna, the kings of Midian, Judges 8:1-6.

Elijah was a prophet and his successor Elisha was very active on both sides of the Jordan River. In 1 Kings 16:29-33 and 1 Kings 17:1-7, God told Elijah to crossover to the east side of the Jordan and hide by the Cherith Brook from King Ahab, after he had given him a prophecy. Elijah had warned King Ahab the king of Israel that there would be a drought in the land because of Israel's evil deeds. The Jordan River became a barrier of protection for Elijah.

In 2 Kings 2:1-18, before Elijah was taken up to heaven, Elijah struck the Jordan River with his cloak, and the water parted so that they could cross the Jordan River. After Elijah had ascended to heaven, Elisha parted the waters with Elijah's cloak so he could return to Israel.

Naaman, a commander of the army of the king of Syria, was healed of leprosy in the Jordan River after he went down and dipped himself seven times, as the prophet Elisha had told him by his messenger, 2 Kings 5:8-15.

Elisha made a borrowed axhead floats on top of the Jordan River by cutting a stick and throwing it into the water, 2 Kings 6:1-7.

In Bible times, the Israelites possessed the territory of both sides of the Jordan. The Israelites crossed the Jordan River into the Promised Land near Jericho. The Israelites were allocated lands from far south of Jerusalem, to far north of the Sea of Galilee. The tribes of Reuben, Gad, and half of Manasseh were given territory east of the Jordan River. Today, the Jordan River creates most of the international boundary between Israel and Jordan.

The Jordan River area was the location where John the Baptist conducted much of his ministry. Jesus Christ was baptized by John the Baptist in the Jordan River. This is also where John the Baptist baptized thousands of people, as did Jesus' disciples.

People from Jerusalem
and from all of Judea and all over the Jordan Valley
went out to see and hear John.
And when they confessed their sins,
he baptized them in the Jordan River.
Matthew 3:5-6 NLT

Jesus crossed the Jordan River during his ministry many times according to Matthew 19:1 and Mark 10:1.

Jesus then left that place and went
into the region of Judea
and across the Jordan.
Again crowds of people came to him,
And as was his custom, he taught them.
Mark 10:1 NIV

The large crowds crossed the Jordan River to come hear Jesus preach and to be healed of their diseases according to Matthew 4:25 and Mark 3:7-8.

Large crowds from Galilee,
the Decapolis, Jerusalem, Judea
and the region across the Jordan followed him.
Matthew 4:25 NIV

The Jordan River is where John the Baptist denies being the Messiah to the priests and Levites, when they asked him who he was, John 1:19-28. The next day John the Baptist bore record of Jesus, as the Son of God and Lamb of God, at the Jordan River, John 1:29-38.

The next day John was there again with two disciples.
When he saw Jesus passing, by,
he said, "Look, the Lamb of God!"
John 1:35-36 NIV

It was near the Jordan River when Andrew and Simon Peter met Jesus, and later became his disciple, John 1:7-43.

When Jesus enemies sought to capture him, Jesus took refuge at the Jordan River at the place John had first baptized him, John 10:39-40.

Out of all the events that took place in, by, near or at the Jordan River, perhaps the most mind-boggling is the baptism of Jesus. Now, what makes that event so special to me? It's not the fact that Jesus was baptized there, but it important.

What touches me is what Father God said to Jesus after he was baptized there.

This is a brief narrative of what happened: Matthew 3:13-16, Jesus came from Galilee to the Jordan to be baptized by John. John tried to stop Jesus. He said, "I need to be baptized by You. Do You come to me?" Jesus said to John, "Let it be done now. We should do what is right." John agreed and baptized Jesus. As soon as Jesus was baptized, and coming out of the water, at that moment heaven was opened, and John saw the Spirit of God descending like a dove and lighting on Jesus. A voice was heard from heaven. It said, "This is My Son, whom I love, with Him, I am well pleased."

My soul rejoices at the pure fact that God, the Father, told Jesus, His son, how very much He loved Him, even before Jesus performed one miracle, preached his first sermon or raised anyone from the dead. Father God loved Jesus, not because of anything he had done or could do, but because Jesus was His Son. Hallelujah! Hallelujah is the highest praise.

Notes of Interest:

<u>The Six Longest Rivers in the United States:</u>

1. Missouri River 2,341 miles
2. Mississippi River 2,202 miles
3. Yukon River 1,979 miles
4. Rio Grande 1,759 miles
5. Colorado River 1,450 miles
6. Arkansas River 1,443 miles

The Three Longest Rivers in the World:

1. The Nile River runs 4,130 miles through ten countries; begins in north-eastern Africa.
2. The Amazon River runs 4,000 miles in South America.
3. The Yangtze River, also called the Chang Jiang River runs 3,988 miles; the longest river in Asia, 3rd longest in the world.

~~~~~~~~~~~~

Chapter 6

BIBLICAL RIVERS

The Arnon River

The Arnon was a roaring river first mentioned in Number 21:24. It serves as the border between Moab and the Amorites and flows through Moab and enters into the Dead Sea. Remember, Moab and Ammon were brothers, children of incest involving Lot and his two daughters, Genesis 19. The oldest daughter named here soon Moab, and the youngest daughter son was named Ben-Ammi also known as Ammon. The Amorites were descended from one of the son of Canaan, Genesis 14:7. The "land of the Amorites" included Syria and Israel.

The Rivers of Damascus

The rivers of Damascus are only mentioned in 2 Kings 5:12. They are named the Abanah and Pharpar rivers. The Abanah flowed through the city of Damascus and the Pharpar just to the south of it. These are the rivers that Naaman with leprosy, ask could he wash in because they were cleaner and better than the water of Israel. In 2 Kings 5, this biblical event took place when Naaman came with his horses and his chariots and stood at the doorway of the house of Elisha. Elisha sent a messenger to tell Naaman to wash in the Jordan River seven times, and his flesh will be restored. But Naaman left furious and made the above statement about the rivers of Damascus are cleaner than the Jordan River. Naaman's servant persuaded him to go and wash. So Naaman went down and dipped himself seven times in the Jordan and his flesh was restored like the flesh of a little child, and he was clean, 2 Kings 5:9-14.

The Euphrates River

In Genesis 2:14 is where the Euphrates Rivers is first mentioned, as one of the four water branches that watered the Garden of Eden. It flows 1,700 miles making it the longest river in Western Asia. From the mountainous region of north-eastern Turkey (Armenia), it flows southward into northern Syria and turns south-easterly to join the Tigris and flows into the Persian Gulf. The Belikh and Khabur are two principal tributaries that flow into the Euphrates from the north. The Tigris and Euphrates rivers regularly form new branches and change their courses. Many battles were fought there, including one in 605 BC between Nebuchadnezzar II of Babylon and Egypt's Pharaoh Necho II. The Towel of Babel was built along this river.

The Habor River

The Habor River was a tributary of the Euphrates. It is mentioned in the 2 Kings 17:6, 2 King 18:11, and 1 Chronicles 5:26. These books of the Bible are often referred to as the Deuteronomistic History, along with Deuteronomy,

Joshua, Judges, 1 & 2 Samuel, 1 Kings and 2 Chronicles. In the ninth year of Hoshea, the king of Assyria captured Samaria and deported Israel to Assyria. He settled them in Halah, in Gozan on the Habor River and in the town of the Medes.

The Jabbok River

The Jabbok is a river east of the Jordan, and it rises in springs near Amman. Amman is the capital of Jordan. It flows through a deep valley westward through Gilead into the Jordan north of the Dead Sea. The river of Jabbok is mentioned in Genesis 32:22, Deuteronomy 3:16, Numbers 21:23-24, and Judges 11:13.

The Jordan River

The Jordon River is at the southern end of Galilee and flows into the Dead Sea. This river is only about eight miles wide and fourteen miles long. It could be crossed without difficulty only at its fords, Joshua 3:1. By controlling the fords during military confrontations in biblical times constituted a critical advantage, Judges 3:38, Judges 12:5-6. The Jordan River served as a boundary, it was always clear that, beyond the Jordan, were residing outside of the Promised Land, Joshua 22:1. This river is mentioned in the Old and New Testaments, Genesis 13:10-11, Genesis 32:9-10, Number 22:1, Joshua 3:14-4:9, 2 Kings 5:8-14, Mark 1:4-5, and Matthew 3:5-6.

The Kebar River (NIV) or The Chebar (KJV)

The Kebar was a river of the Euphrates in Babylon where the exiles gathered to pray. In the days of Ezekiel, Israel had turned away from God, and in 605 BC, Babylon defeated Judah, putting the nation under their control. The Kebar River is only mentioned in the Old Testament, and only in the book of Ezekiel. It is mentioned 8 times in the following chapters and verses; Ezekiel 1:1, Ezekiel 1:3, Ezekiel 3:15, Ezekiel 3:23, Ezekiel 10:15, Ezekiel 10:20, Ezekiel 10:22, and Ezekiel 43:3.

In my thirtieth year,
in the fourth month of the fifth day,
while I was among the exiles by the Kebar River,
the heavens were opened and I saw visions of God.
Ezekiel 1:1 NIV

The Kishon River

The Kishon flowed northwest across the Plain of Megiddo and could quickly flood as a result of storms. This river is mentioned in Judges 5:21 and Psalm 83:9. In biblical history, it is best known from Barak and Deborah victory over the Canaanites forces of Sisera, Judges 4 & 5. 1 Kings 18:1-40, Elijah's contest with the prophets of Baal on Mount Carmel took place around the Kishon River.

The Tigris River

The Tigris River is also called Hiddekel in Genesis 2:14. This river is mentioned in Genesis 2:14, Daniel 10:4-5, and

Nahum 2:6-8. It reaches flood stage during March and April and subsides after mid-May. The bank of the Tigris is where some of the most famous cities of antiquity reigned, which are listed below.

1. Nineveh, capital of Assyria during the Assyrian Empire
2. Asshur, the original capital of Assyria
3. Ctesihyphon, capital of the Parthians and Sassanians
4. Seleucia, capital of the Seleucid Empire

The Marah River

The Marah River is the first body of water encountered after the Israelites crossed the divided Red Sea by the Lord on a dry seabed on foot. The water was bitter and undrinkable until Moses threw a particular tree into the river pointed out by the Lord, and then the water became sweet and drinkable, Exodus 13:23-25. After 40 years of wandering in the desert, it was Joshua who led the children of Israel across the Jordan River into the land that God had promised Moses, Joshua 1:1-9.

The Orontes River

The Orontes River is a river of Lebanon, Syria, and Turkey. It is also known as Al- Assi River, Draco, Typhon, and Axius. It was famous for the battle of Kadesh during the reign of Ramesses II; 1279-1213 BC. Two other battles fought at the river were "The Battle of Qarqar" fought in 853 BC, and in 637 AD, "The Battle of Iron Bridge" between the forces of Rashidum Caliphate and Byzantine Empire. The

Orontes has long been a boundary marker. Its river source is the springs of The Bequaa Valley in east Lebanon. It rises in the Anti-Libanus, flowing past Antioch, and falling into the sea at the foot of Mount Pieria.

Yarkon River

The Yarkon River is formed by the seasonal runoff from the western slopes of the Samaritan and Judean hills that flow into the Kanah Brook. The Yarkon historically created a significant barrier to the north and south traffic because of the extensive swamps that formed along its course. The Yarkon River in biblical times established the border between the tribes of Dan and Ephraim to the north. The Kanah Brook established the boundary between the tribe of Ephraim and Manasseh, Joshua 17:9.

Chapter 7

SEAS

Bible's seas are listed in this chapter. I noticed when researching these seas that the same sea might be called by another name depending on the Bible translation. A good example of this would be Genesis 14:3; listed below is that particular verse in four different Bible translation styles.

KJV - All these were joined together in the vale of Siddim, which is the salt sea.
NIV - All these latter kings joined forces in the Valley of Siddim (that is, the Dead Sea Valley).
NLT - The second group of kings joined forces in Siddim Valley (that is, the valley of the Dead Sea).
TLB - These kings (of Sodom, Gomorrah, Admah, Zeboiim, and Bela) mobilized their armies in Siddim Valley (that is, the valley of the Dead Sea).

The Sea of Galilee, the Red Sea, the Dead Sea, the Mediterranean Sea, and the Jordan River are used as geographical boundaries for the land of Canaan. These bodies of water served as boundaries of the allotted inheritance land of the Israelites when they enter Canaan, God spoke the instruction to Moses, Numbers 34:1-15.

The Sea of Galilee is one of Israel's largest freshwater sources, about 33 miles around, 13 miles long and 8 miles wide. The

Sea of Galilee lies low in the Great Rift Valley, surrounded by hills which make it is prone to sudden turbulence storms. Storms of this kind were a hazard for Galilee fishermen, but Mark records Jesus calming a storm of this nature, Mark 4:35-41. The Sea of Galilee is also known by several names listed below.

1. Sea of Tiberias   John 6:1, John 21:1
2. Sea of Chinneroth   Joshua 12:3
3. Sea of Chinnereth   Joshua 13:27, Numbers 34:11

Many events during Jesus' ministry happened at the Sea of Galilee. Jesus made the fishing town of Capernaum the center of his ministry in Galilee. When Jesus heard that John had been arrested, he left Judea and returned to Galilee. He went first to Nazareth, then left there and moved to Capernaum, beside the Sea of Galilee, in the region of Zebulun and Naphtali, Mathew 4:12-14.

One day, while Jesus was walking along the shore of the Sea of Galilee, he saw two brothers named Simon and Andrew. They were throwing a net into the water, for they fished for a living. Jesus called out to them, "Come, follow me, and I will show you how to fish for people! And they left their nets at once and followed him, Matthew 4:18-20.

Question: What is the other name Jesus called Andrew's brother Simon?

Answer in back of book

A little farther up the shore of Galilee, Jesus saw two other brothers, named James and John. They were sitting in a boat with their father, Zebedee, repairing their nets. Jesus called them to follow him, too. They immediately followed Jesus, leaving the boat and their father behind, Matthew 4:21-22.

Notes of Interest: There are approximately 27 species of fish in the Sea of Galilee. One fish is nicknamed St. Peter's Fish. This fish belongs to a species named Genus Tilapia. Its Arabic name "musht" means "comb" refers to it comb-like tail. The nickname St. Peter's fish relates to the Gospel of Matthew 17:24-27. The Temple Tax Collector asked Peter where Jesus going to pays the Temple tax. Jesus tells Peter to go to the sea, cast a hook and take the first fish that comes up. Jesus also tells Peter when he opens the fish mouth, he will find a coin, and take that coin and give it to Temple Tax Collector for them. The temple tax was a tax which went towards the upkeep of the Jewish Temple. Each man who is at least 20 years or older was to give to the Lord this offering which was ½ shekel of silver. It is impossible to know the silver value in biblical times for ½ shekel of silver but at today's rate it around five dollars.

~~~~~~~~~~~~

Jesus was met by two men possessed by demons, and he healed them after he arrived on the other side of the Sea of Galilee, in the region of the Gadarenes, Matthew 8:28-34.

When Jesus crossed the far side of the Sea of Galilee, also known as the Sea of Tiberias, a huge crowd kept following him because they saw his miraculous signs as he healed the sick, John 6:1-4.

The Red Sea is mentioned first in Exodus 13:18.
So God led the people around by the
desert road toward the Red Sea.
The Israelites went up out of Egypt ready for battle.
Exodus 13:18 NIV

There are several reasons why it's called the Red Sea. The first reason is because of a type of algae called Trichodesmium Erythraeum. When the algae's blooms die off, they appear to turn the blue-green color of the water to a reddish-brown and floats near the top of the water. The second reason is that in ancient Mediterranean times, directions were referred to as colors; black, red, green and white. The color black relates to the North, red refers to the South, green refers to the East and white to the West. The Red Sea was located in the south and was often referred to as the sea of the south, or the Red Sea.

The Dead Sea is about 9.5 miles wide and 48 miles long. It's the lowest place on earth, the hottest spot in Israel, and nothing visible can live in its waters when salt content is 35%. In the wakes of rainy winters, the Dead Sea temporarily comes to life. The water from the Jordan River flows into it from the base of Mount Hermon and empties into the Dead Sea just south of Jericho. There is no outlet, and minerals including salt, gather and remain in the dense water, making it unsuitable to support life. Throughout history, the Dead Sea is known by several names. The Bible Scriptures refers to it as the Salt Sea in Number 34:3, the Sea in Ezekiel 47:8 and the Eastern Sea in Joel 2:20.

The region used to be a well-watered area, as fruitful and beautiful as the Garden of Eden. God's judgment on Sodom and Gomorrah changed the area's fertility to a desolate place that represented the judgment on sin; Genesis 13:10, Deuteronomy 29:23 and Jeremiah 17:6. The evaporation hovering over the surface of the Dead Sea gives it a dull cloudy appearance; it resembles a furnace-like smoke that rose from the valley after the destruction of Sodom, Genesis 19:28.

The Mediterranean Sea is known by several names in the Bible.

1. Great Sea in Numbers 34:6 (KJV)
2. Sea of the Philistines in Exodus 23:31 (KJV)
3. Sea in Deuteronomy 11:23, Deuteronomy 34:2, Zechariah 14:8 (KJV)

The Mediterranean Sea was considered the crossroads of the earth in ancient times. It's approximately 2,300 miles long and touches upon Europe, Africa, and Asia. Many ancient Bible civilizations were connected with the Mediterranean Sea including Phoenicia, Tyre, Egypt, Rome, Greece, and Philistia. King Solomon had Cedars of Lebanon floated on rafts down the Mediterranean Sea coast which were used for the construction of the Temple, 1 Kings 5:9. The Apostle Paul traveled extensively over the Mediterranean Sea during his missionary journeys to Antioch of Pisidia, Corinth, Ephesus, and Rome.

<u>The Sea of the Arabah</u> is mentioned in Joshua 12:3. It's a geographic name for the area south of the Dead Sea basin. It also forms part of the border between Israel to the west and Jordan to the east. The Sea of the Arabah is one of the areas where Israel won the battle over the Kings in the land. There was a total of 31 kings Israel defeated, and the land they conquer included the hill country, the western foothills, the Arabah, the mountain slopes, the wilderness and the Negev, Joshua 12:8-24.

<u>The Egyptian Sea</u> is only mentioned once in the Bible, Isaiah 11:15.

> **The Lord will dry up the gulf of the Egyptians sea;**
> **with a scorching wind he will sweep his**
> **hand over the Euphrates River.**
> **He will break it up into seven streams**
> **so that anyone can cross in sandals.**
> Isaiah 11:15 NIV

<u>The Adriatic or Sea of Adria</u>

> **On the fourteenth night**
> **we were still being driven across the Adriatic Sea,**
> **when about midnight the sailors sensed**
> **they were approaching land.**
> Acts 27:27 NIV

The Adria Sea in the King James Bible also called the Adriatic Sea in the New International Bible Version, is only mentioned in the above verse. It's in regards to the "Sail, Storm, Shipwreck and Safety of Paul," Acts 27:1-44.

The Sea of Joppa is only mentioned in Ezra 3:7. The Hebrew word for "Joppa" means "beautiful." Joppa has served as Israel's seaport for trade since ancient Bible times. The Lebanon cedar that was used in the original Temple of Jerusalem arrived at Joppa, by sea from Tyre. Apostle Peter raised Tabitha back to life at Joppa, Acts 9:36-42.

The Sea of Jazer marked the boundary of the Ammonites, Numbers 21:24. It was also occupied by the tribe of Gad, Number 32:1.

Chapter 8

BROOKS

Remember, a brook is a natural stream of water smaller than a river, and often a tributary of a river? A collection of verses mostly from the KJV, in regards to Brooks, are listed below.

1.   Brooks of Arnon   Numbers 21:14-15 KJV

Wherefore it is said in the book of the wars of the Lord, What he did in the Red Sea, and in the brooks of Arnon, And at the stream of the brooks that goeth down to the dwelling of Ar, and lieth upon the border of Moab.

This verse is referring to places where victories by the Lord took place for the Israelites. The brooks of Arnon were named as one.

2.   Brook Besor   1 Samuel 30:9-10 KJV

So, David went, he and the six hundred men that were with him, and came to the brook Besor, where those that were left behind stayed. But David pursued, he and four hundred men: for two hundred abodes behind, which were so faint that they could not go over the brook Besor.

This brook is in the far southwest of Judah. This is the place where 200 of David's men stayed behind because they were faint, while the other 400 pursued the Amalekites. The Amalekites had raided the town Ziklag in the region of Negev. They had taken captive all the women, which included the wives of David and the men of his army.

3.   Brook Cedron/Kidron   John 18:1 KJV

When Jesus had spoken these words, he went forth with his disciples over the brook Cedron, where was a garden, into which he entered, and is disciples.

Jesus and his disciples crossed the Cedron Brook on their way to the Garden of Gethsemane. Judas the same night betrayed Jesus. He brought a company of soldiers and some guards that arrested Jesus there.

4.   Brook Cherith   1 Kings 17:3-5 KJV

Get thee hence, and turn thee eastward, and hide thyself by the brook Cherith that is before Jordan. And it shall be, thou shalt drink of the brook; and I have commanded the ravens to feed thee there. So he went and did according unto the word of the Lord: for he went and dwelt by the brook Cherith that is before Jordan.

This is the brook where Elijah was fed by ravens. They brought him bread and meat in the morning and in the evening, and Elijah drank from this brook. After Elijah had spoken to King Ahab, telling him that neither dew nor rain will come to the land for the next 3 ½ years, except at his word. Instantly, the word of the Lord came to Elijah and told him to flee to the brook of Cherith and hide there.

5.   Brook of Eshcol   Numbers 13:23-24 KJV

And they came unto the brook of Eshcol, and cut down from thence a branch with one cluster of grapes, and they bare it between two upon a staff; and they brought of the pomegranates, and of the figs. The place was called the brook Eshcol, because of the cluster of grapes which the children of Israel cut down from thence.

Moses sent twelve spies to the land that was promised to his forefathers, he asked them to bring information concerning the area. Out of the twelve spies only two returned with good news; Aaron, and Caleb. The brook of Eshcol is where the spies brought some fruits from the Promised Land back to their people.

6.a.   Brooks of Gaash   2 Samuel 23:30 KJV
Benaiah the Pirathonite, Hiddai of the brooks of Gaash.

In these verses, 2 Samuel 23:8-39, David is identifying his mightiest warriors and where they come from. The warrior Hiddai is an Israelite from the brooks of Gaash located in the southwestern hills of Israel.

6.b.   Brooks of Gaash   1 Chronicles 11:32 KJV
Hurai of the brooks of Gaash, Abiel the Arbathite.

In 1 Chronicles 11:1-9, David becomes the king of Israel and Judah. In verses 10-47, David names his strong men of the armies. One of his strong men is called Hurai of the brooks of Gaash.

7.   Jokneam Brook   Joshua 19:11 NIV

From there it circled to the west, going near Maralah and Dabbesheth until it reached the brook east of Jokneam.

This verse describes the third allotment of land that was given to the clans of the tribe of Zebulun which started at Sarid. Zebulun was the tenth son of Jacob and the last of six sons by Leah.

8.a.   Brook Kidron   2 Samuel 15:23 KJV

And all the country wept with a loud voice, and all the people passed over: the king also himself passed over the brook Kidron, and all the people passed over, toward the way of the wilderness.

This verse referred to David when he fled Jerusalem because the majority of Israel had joined his son, Absalom in a conspiracy against him. The whole countryside wept aloud, as all the people passed by carrying the ark of the covenant of God. Zadok, the priest and all the Levites came along with King David. Abiathar, the priest, offered sacrifices until everyone had passed out of the city, and over the Brook Kidron.

8.b.   Brook Kidron   1 Kings 15:13 KJV

And also Maachah his mother, even her he removed from being queen because she had made an idol in a grove; and Asa destroyed her idol, and burnt it by the brook Kidron.

This verse is referring to what King Asa took from his mother, the queen for worshipping idol gods. He destroyed his mother's idols and burnt them by the Kidron Brook.

8.c.   Brook Kidron   John 18:1 KJV

When Jesus had spoken these words, he went forth with his disciples over the brook Cedron, (KJV) and Kidron (NIV) where was a garden, into the which he entered, and his disciples.

After Jesus had finished praying to his father in chapter 17; He and his disciples crossed over the Cedron Brook to go to the Garden of Gethsemane. John 17 is the longest recorded prayer of Jesus and found only in John. In that prayer, Jesus prays to be glorified, prays for His disciples, and prays for all Believers.

9.a.   Brook of Kishon/Kison   Psalms 83:9 KJV

Do unto them as unto the Midianites; as to Sisera, as to Jabin, at the brook of Kison:

This is a verse from the prayer for the defeat of Israel's enemies. The Midianites conspired with the Moabites to curse Israel, but the curse was turned into a blessing instead. Jael is the Kenite woman who slew Sisera the commander of the Canaanite army, after inviting him into her tent to sleep.

9.b.   Brook of Kishon/Kison   1Kings 18:40 KJV

And Elijah said unto them, Take the prophets of Baal; let not one of them escape. And they took them: and Elijah brought them down to the brook Kishon, and slew them there.

Elijah challenges 450 prophets of Baal to a contest at the altar on Mount Carmel to prove that Israel's God is the "Only True Living God." The prophets of Baal would call on their false gods and Elijah would call on the Lord God. Whoever answered by fire would be considered the True Living God. The prophets of Baal took their bull and prepared it as a sacrifice on an altar. They began to call out to Baal for hours; there was no answer. Elijah took twelve stones to represent the 12 tribes of Israel. He built an altar, made a trench around the altar and filled it with seed. Elijah then put the wood on the altar with the sacrifice on top. Next, Elijah asked for four water pots to be poured on the altar sacrifice, and this was done 3 times; that's a total of 12 pots of water. Elijah spoke a simple prayer to the Lord. Immediately, fire fell from heaven and consumed the sacrifice. The people fell on their face. Elijah then told them to kill the prophets of Baal and don't let none of them escape.

10.   Shihor Brook   Joshua 19:26 NKJV

Alammelech, Amad, and Mishal; it reached to Mount Carmel westward, along the Brook Shihor Libnath.

This verse refers to the fifth area of land allotted to the tribe of Asher. It tells and describes the area which included the

Shihor Brook. Asher was the 8th son of Jacob and his 2nd son by Zilpah; their 1st son together was named Gad. Zilpah was Leah's maidservant.

11.   Brook of the Willows   Isaiah 15:7 KJV

Therefore the abundance they have gotten, and that which they have laid up, shall they carry away to the Brook of the Willows.

A prophecy against Moab consists of 9 verses, in which the above verse is one of them. The lamentations were heard through the country of Moab when they became a prey to the Assyrian army.

12.   Zered Brook   Deuteronomy 2:13-14 KJV

Now rise up, said I, and get you over the brook Zered. And we went over the brook Zered. And the space in which we came from Kadeshbarnea until we were come over the brook Zered, was thirty and eight years; until all the generation of the men of war were wasted out from among the host, as the Lord sware unto them.

Brook Zered is mentioned three times in two verses, only in Deuteronomy 2. This verse refers to the Israelites wanderings in the wilderness. It took them thirty-eight years to finally get across the Zered Brook from Kadesh. Moses' brother Aaron helped the people make a golden calf which they worship, Exodus 32. Israelites broke their original covenant with God. God swore that the first generation would never enter the Promised Land, except for two faithful men,

Numbers 14. The Israelites wander in the wilderness until the first generation died. The second generation of Israel inherited the Promised Land, Joshua 10.

> **All these kings and their lands Joshua**
> **conquered in one campaign,**
> **because the Lord, the God of Israel,**
> **fought for Israel.**
> Joshua 10:42 NIV

By the way, the two faithful men were Caleb, son of Jephunneh and Joshua, son of Nun, Numbers 14:30.

In closing this chapter . . .

> **The words of a man's mouth**
> **are as deep waters,**
> **and the wellspring of wisdom**
> **as a flowing brook.**
> Proverbs 18:4 KJV

Wise words are like deep waters;
wisdom flows from the wise like a bubbling brook.
Proverbs 18:4 NLT

Chapter 9

BIBLICAL HISTORY

The first part of Bible history begins with the creation of the universe to Abraham. This period takes place from creation to 2000 BC, and it is recorded in the first eleven chapters of Genesis. It consists of the following:

1. The creation of heaven and earth, Genesis 1
2. The creation of man
3. Description of the four rivers in the Garden of Eden
   Let's name them, right quick . . . smile

   1. _____
   2. _____
   3. _____
   4. _____

   Answer in Chapter 2

4. Woman made from the rib of man
5. The fall of man
6. The murder of Abel by Cain
7. Noah and the Flood
8. The Tower of Babel in the land of Shinar, Genesis 11

Next, the time period of Abraham to Moses takes place between 2000 – 1500 BC. In this era the experience of one man, Abraham is primarily recorded. It traces out the history of his descendant until they become a nation in Egypt. The record set forth the life event of Isaac, the son of Abraham, and Isaac's son, Jacob. It also deals at considerable length with Jacob's sons, especially Joseph, who delivered his father's family from famine by bringing them into Egypt. The period is recorded in Genesis 12 -50. In Chapter 41, the Nile River is mentioned. Pharaoh dreamt that he was standing by the Nile River when he saw seven thin cows eat seven healthy and fat cows.

The Exodus period is 1500 – 1450 BC. After the death of Joseph, the Israelites, God's chosen people grew into a nation in Egypt. The Egyptians became fearful of them and enslaved them. Moses was raised up as an Egyptian and trained for forty years in Egypt. When he feared for his life, he lived forty years on the backside of the Sinai desert. Under the leadership of Moses, the Children of Israel departed Egypt, crossed the Red Sea on dry land after God divided it and sent a strong east wind to dry the riverbed. Israelites then spend approximately 40 years wandering in the wilderness. At last, upon the death of Moses, Joshua led them into Canaan. This era is recorded in Exodus, Leviticus, Numbers, and Deuteronomy. The Marah River is the first body of water encountered after the Israelites crossed the divided Red Sea by the Lord on a dry seabed on foot. The water was bitter and undrinkable until Moses threw a particular tree into the river, Exodus 13. Also, during this era, the River Arnon and Jabbok Rivers are mentioned in Deuteronomy 2, verses 36 and 37.

The Conquest of Canaan occurs between 1460 – 1450 BC. Joshua led Israel on dry land over the Jordan River, and by a series of battles defeated the inhabitants of Canaan. Joshua and the Israelites pierced to the center of the territory and through the conquest of Jericho and Ai. They swept south, defeating the allied kings and later invaded the northern section. When the inhabitants were reduced, Joshua divided the land among the Twelve Tribes of Israel. This period is recorded in the book of Joshua. The Euphrates, Arnon, Jabbok, and the River of Egypt are mentioned in this book.

The Judges era begins in 1450 and ends in 1102 BC During this time the Israelites came upon the miserable days of the Judges. This was a time of failure and defeat. During this period Israel had no stable government, no central capital, a cycle of sin and deliverance. On many occasions, God raised up Judges who were military leaders that rule over them, saved and delivered them from their plunderers. These biblical events are found in the books of Judges and Ruth. In the book of Judges, the Kishon River is mentioned in three verses.

The Kingdom period began in 1102 and lasted until 982 BC. Samuel the last of the Judges of Israel was also a prophet. He anointed Saul as the first king of Israel. During the reign of King Saul, David and Solomon the Israelites attained their highest glory. Their government was firmly established, their arts and architecture flourished. Israel's borders were pushed out to the river of Egypt in one direction, and to the Euphrates in the other. This period is recorded in 1 and 2 Samuel, 1 and 2 Kings and 1 and 2 Chronicles. The rivers of Damascus are first mentioned during this time period, along with the river of Gozan.

Let's name the two rivers of Damascus, right quick . . . smile

    1. _A_____

    2. _P_____

Answer in Chapter 6

The Northern Kingdom 722 – 587 BC

Israel was the Northern Kingdom, and it was conquered by the Assyrians around 722 BC, and the people were carried captive to Assyria. Judah was the Southern Kingdom which stood for one hundred and thirty-five years, after the fall of Israel. Judah's kings had shown more loyalty to the Lord. This period is recorded in 1 and 2 Samuel, 1 and 2 Kings and 1 and 2 Chronicles.

The Kingdom of Judah's Captivity 587 – 538 BC

The Kingdom of Judah, in spite of the warnings of the prophets, went deeper and deeper into sin and idolatry. God gave them over to King Nebuchadnezzar, and he carried them away as captivities to Babylon. The city and the Temple which had been their pride and glory were burned to the ground. These are the Israelites, who had marched on dry-shod in triumph over the Jordan River to the promised land, Canaan; now they are marched away in chains. This period is recorded in 1 and 2 Samuel, 1 and 2 Kings and 1 and 2 Chronicles.

The Restoration 538 – 391 BC

Jerusalem was in ruins, and it people was in captivity. Cyrus, upon his accession to the throne, issued a decree permitting the people to return and rebuild their city and their Temple. Under Zerubbabel, about 42,360 Jews made their way back to the Jerusalem to re-establish themselves in the land of their forefathers. This era is found in the books of Ezra, Nehemiah, and Esther.

A period of about 400 years took place between the Old and New Testaments; 391- 5 BC. The Old Testament ends with the restoration and re-establishment. The Jews passed through various stages, experience, and their language and customs changed. The Israelites in Christ's day were very different from the people who lived in the days of Ezra and Nehemiah.

Life of Christ 5 BC to 28 AD

After the long silence of four hundred years, the voice of God was heard. John the Baptist started preaching in the wilderness of Judea, preparing the way for the Messiah. The Messiah came, was baptized in the Jordan River by John the Baptist, manifested himself to the people, and was rejected, and then crucified by his own people. The record of this biblical event is recorded in Matthew, Mark, Luke, and John.

The Spread of the Gospel 28 – 100 AD

While the Old Testament covers about 3500 years, the New Testament covers less than 100 years. After the life of Jesus is recorded in the Gospels, we have the Acts and Epistles that give an account of the spread of the gospel. For a time, the Gospel flourished in Jerusalem. Then the Gospel went on its way through Judea and Samaria to the remote parts of the earth. It was by a river in the book of Acts that Paul and his followers met a woman named Lydia. She was from the city of Thyatira, a dealer of purple who became their first convert in Europe after hearing the word of God.

> **On the Sabbath we went outside of**
> **the city gate to the river,**
> **where we expected to find a place of prayer.**
> **We sat down and began to speak to the**
> **women who had gathered there.**
> **One of those listening was a woman**
> **from the city of Thyatira**
> **named Lydia, a dealer in purple cloth.**
> **She was a worshiper of God.**
> **The Lord opened her heart to**
> **respond to Paul's message.**
> **When she and the members of her**
> **household were baptized,**
> **she invited us to her home.**
> Acts 16: 13-15 NIV

Notes of Interest:

Seas of the Old Testament World

1. The Red Sea
2. The Mediterranean Sea also called the Great Sea

3. The Dead Sea also called the Sea of the Plain, the Salt Sea
4. The Sea of Galilee also known as the Sea of Tiberias, and the Sea of Chinnereth
5. The Sea of Arabah
6. The Sea of Egyptian
7. The Sea of Jazer
8. The Sea of Joppa
9. The Sea of Adriatic

The Great Mountains in the Old Testament World

1. Mt. Ararat is where Noah's Ark rested on one of the mountain peaks after the waters of the flood subsided.
2. Mt. Carmel is the location of the scene of Elijah's sacrifice.
3. Mt. Ebal is where the stones inscribed with the Law were deposited.
4. Mt. Gerizim is where the Samaritans hold their Passover.
5. Mt. Gilboa is the place of Saul and Jonathan's death.
6. Mt. Gilead is a mountain region east of Jordan. It is where the covenant between Laban and Jacob took place.
7. Mt. Horeb was the location of the burning bush. It's where Israelites encamped for nearly a yearly, and where the Law was given to Moses. It is also where Elijah heard a still, small voice. Mt. Horeb is also known as Mt. Sinai.

8. Mt. Lebanon is the source for the timber for Solomon's Temple and is located in the central mountains of Syria.

9. Mt. Moriah is the site of Abraham's intended sacrifice and the mountain on which the Temple of Jerusalem was built.

10. The Mount of Olives also referred to as Mt. Olives. It is the place of David's flight from Absalom; of Jesus' weeping over Jerusalem; and of Jesus Ascension.

11. Mt. Pisgah is where Moses climbed to the top, and there the Lord showed him the Promised Land.

12. Mt. Zion is the eastern hill of Jerusalem. It was the stronghold of the Jebusites a Canaanite Tribe, attacked by Joab and became the site of David's palace and the Temple.

The Countries of the Old Testament World were divided into three Divisions

1. The Countries of the Eastern Slope:
   Armenia
   Media
   Persia

2. The Countries of the Tigris and Euphrates:
   Assyria
   Elam
   Mesopotamia
   Chaldea
   Arabia

3. The Western Countries of the Mediterranean:
   Asia Minor

Syria
Phoenicia
Canaan
The Wilderness
Egypt

The Ten Important Cities of the Old Testament World

1. Nineveh is the capital of ancient Assyrian, Genesis 10:11.
2. Susa is the capital of the Persian Empire. It's where King Ahasuerus sat on his royal throne in the book of Ester 1:1-3.
3. Haran located in Mesopotamia is Abram's first camping place, Genesis 11:31.
4. Babylon is the capital of Chaldea.
5. Ur is located on the Euphrates River, and the home of Terah; Abraham's father.
6. Damascus is the capital of Syria and the oldest and largest city.
7. Sidon in Phoenicia, also called Saida was named after the firstborn son of Canaan, Genesis 10:15. Later Joshua included it as part of the land promised to Israel, Joshua 13:6
8. The city of Tyre in Phoenicia is 20 miles south of Sidon. It was the commercial seaport of that country. Tyre was part of Asher's western boundary mentioned in Joshua 19:29.
9. Jerusalem, the capital of Israel.
10. Memphis, the early capital of Egypt.

~~~~~~~~~~~~

A Reader's Question

This new section just dropped in my spirit at 0613 on January 14, 2017, titled A Reader's Question.

An individual asked me a question similar to this, why do I put "Notes of Interest" throughout the books. She also stated that she likes them.

<u>The Answer</u>:

The "truth of the matter" is that "Notes of Interest" comes from one of the following:

1. A word(s) or name that grabs my attention.
2. Something that I desire to know more about.
3. While researching, I ran across something that I thought would be interesting to share with others.

Author's Closing Remarks

In the beginning, God created the heaven and the earth. And the earth was without form and void, and darkness was upon the face of the deep. And the Spirit of God moved upon the face of the waters, Genesis 1:1-2.

Day 1:   God created light and divided it from the darkness.

Day 2:   God separated the sky from the waters.

Day 3   God gathered the waters under the heaven and let the dry land appear. The dry land was called "earth" and the gathering together of the waters he called "seas." Then God said, let the earth grow plant life, each according to its kind throughout the earth.

Day 4:   God created the sun, moon, and stars.

Day 5:   God created the birds of the air, fishes and other living creatures in the seas.

Day 6:   God created all the land animals and man.

Day 7:   God rested.

The word "water(s)" flows through the beginning of the Bible, to the end of the Bible; Revelation 22:17. The first time "waters" is mentioned is in Genesis 1:2. Note, before anything was created, there were waters. These waters were called "seas" by God, Genesis 1:10. This is the only body of water in the Bible that God name.

The first time "river" is mentioned is in the Garden of Eden, Genesis 2:10.

> **And a river went out of Eden to water the garden;**
> **and from thence it was parted,**
> **and became into four heads.**
> Genesis 2:10 KJV

Pray for the Ministry . . . May the "LORD of Peace," give you His Peace.

Dr. Vanessa

References

Chapter 1   Streams & Rivers

1.   Wikipedia, The Free Encyclopedia: https://en.wikipedia. org/wiki/Watercourse

Chapter 2   The Garden of Eden

1.   Wikipedia, The Free Encyclopedia: https://en.wikipedia. org/wiki/Garden_of_Eden
2.   Wikipedia, The Free Encyclopedia: https//:en.wikipedia. org/wiki/Gihon_River

Chapter 3   Wadi

1.   Wikipedia, The Free Encyclopedia: https://en.wikipedia. org/wiki/Estuary
2.   Wikipedia, The Free Encyclopedia: https://en.wikipedia. org/wiki/River
3.   Wikipedia, The Free Encyclopedia: https://en.wikipedia. org/wiki/Anabranch
4.   Wikipedia, The Free Encyclopedia: https://en.wikipedia. org/wiki/Amman

Chapter 4   The Nile River

1.   BibleGateway: https://www.biblegateway.com
2.   Egypt and the Bible http://www.biblearchaeology.org/ post/2008/07/26/Egypt-and-the-Bible

3. The Blue Nile River https://allafricafacts.com/the-blue-nile-river

Chapter 5   The Jordan River

1. BibleGateway: https://www.biblegateway.com
2. Wikipedia, The Free Encyclopedia: https://en.wikipedia.org/wiki/Jordan-River

Chapter 6   Biblical Rivers

1. BibleGateway: https://www.biblegateway.com
2. Rivers and Waterways in the Bible: https://www.studylights.org/dictionaries/hbd/r/rivers-and-waterways-in-the-bible

Chapter 7   Seas

1. Wikipedia, The Free Encyclopedia: https://en.wikipedia.org/wiki/Seas

Chapter 8   Brooks

1. BibleGateway: https://www.biblegateway.com
2. Wikipedia, The Free Encyclopedia: https://en.wikipedia.org/wiki/Brooks

Chapter 9   Biblical History

1. Map of the Old Testament World: https://www.bible-history.com/maps/3-old-testament-world.html
2. Daughters of Zion all Women's Bible College
3. Jacksonville Theological Seminary

Answers & Information Section

Chapter 1
The Oceans are listed from largest to smallest

1. Pacific Ocean
2. Atlantic Ocean
3. Indian Ocean
4. Arctic Ocean

Chapter 3
The 22 Arab Countries

1. Algeria
2. Bahrain
3. Comoros
4. Djibouti
5. **Egypt**
6. Iraq
7. **Jordan**
8. Kuwait
9. **Lebanon**
10. **Libya**
11. Mauritania
12. Morocco
13. Oman
14. **Palestine**
15. Qatar
16. Saudi Arabia
17. Somalia

18. Sudan
19. **Syria**
20. Tunisia
21. The United Arab Emirates
22. Yemen

<u>Chapter 4</u>
The Ten Plagues

1. The Nile River turned to Blood, Exodus 7:14-25
2. Frogs, Exodus 8:1-15
3. Gnats, Exodus 8:16-19
4. Flies, Exodus 8:20-32
5. Death of Livestock, Exodus 9:1-7
6. Boils, Exodus 9:8-12
7. Hail, 9:13-35
8. Locusts, Exodus 10:1-20
9. Darkness, Exodus 10:21-29
10. Death of the Firstborn, Exodus 11:1 – 12:30

<u>The Egyptian Gods or Goddesses attacked by the Plagues:</u>

1. The Nile River turned to Blood
   a. Hapi/Apis, the bull god and the god of the Nile
   b. Isis, the goddess of the Nile
   c. Khnum, the ram god guardian of the Nile
2. Frogs
   a. Heqet, the goddess of birth with a frog head
3. Gnats
   a. Set, the god of the desert
4. Files
   a. Re is a sun god

    b.   Uatchit is represented by the fly
5. Death of Livestock
    a.   Hathor is the goddess with the cow head
    b.   Apis, the bull god is a symbol of fertility
6. Boils
    a.   Sekhmet, the goodness with power over disease
    b.   Sunu is the pestilence god
    c.   Isis is the goddess of healing
7. Hail
    a.   Nut is the sky goddess
    b.   Osiris is the god of crops and fertility
    c.   Set is the god of storms
8. Locusts
    a.   Nut, the sky goddess
    b.   Osiris is the god of crops and fertility
9. Darkness
    a.   Re, the sun god
    b.   Horus is a sun god
    c.   Nut is a sky goddess
    d.   Hathor is a sky goddess
10. Death of the Firstborn
    a.   Min is the god of reproduction
    b.   Heqet is the goddess who attended women at childbirth
    c.   Isis is the goddess who protected children
    d.   Pharaoh's first son is a god

Who were Moses' biological parents?

Amram a Levite was the father of Moses. Moses' mother was named Jochebed, a daughter of the Levi (the third son of

Jacob and Leah) and also the mother of Aaron and Miriam. She was the wife of Amram, as well as his aunt.

Chapter 7

What is the other name Jesus called Andrew's brother Simon? Peter - Matthew 16:18 & John 1:42

About the Book

The twelfth book in a series titled Isaiah 26:3–4, Perfect Peace. What are some of the most important rivers in the Bible? Do you know the difference between a river, stream, or brook? What awesome Bible events took place at these bodies of water? If you don't know the answers to these questions, this book will help you answer these questions and will share unique information regarding the Bible.

About the Author

Vanessa Rayner is a passionate writer. Who writes biblical events and data in an "Unique and Profound" manner. She is dedicated in fulfilling the manifestation of God's work for her life. She is church raised, God appointed, and man-made certified. Vanessa Rayner received her doctor's degree from Jacksonville Theological Seminary.

Other Books by the Author

From the Pew to the Pulpit Published: 08/29/2007

Isaiah 26:3-4 "Perfect Peace" Published: 09/07/2010

Isaiah 26:3-4 "Perfect Peace" Published: 02/13/2012
The Last Single Digit

Isaiah 26:3-4 "Perfect Peace III" Published: 10/24/2012
Silver and Gold

Isaiah 26:3-4 "Perfect Peace IV" Published: 04/10/2013
The Kingdom Number

Isaiah 26:3-4 "Perfect Peace V" Published: 09/06/2013
2541

Isaiah 26:3-4 "Perfect Peace VI" Published: 02/28/2014
Zacchaeus

Isaiah 26:3-4 "Perfect Peace VII" Published: 10/29/2014
Eleven

Isaiah 26:3-4 "Perfect Peace Published: 05/22/2015
VIII" Prayer

Isaiah 26:3-4 "Perfect Peace IX" Published: 10/26/2015
Sixteen

Isaiah 26:3-4 "Perfect Peace X" Published: 04/12/2016
Dreams

Isaiah 26:3-4 "Perfect Peace XI" Published: 02/13/2017
Door

Printed in the United States
By Bookmasters